Quick Mea. ... u. Mug Recipes That Are Too Delicious

Prepare Your Meals in Just 5 Minutes

BY: Valeria Ray

License Notes

A Special Reward for Purchasing My Book!

Thank you, cherished reader, for purchasing my book and taking the time to read it. As a special reward for your decision, I would like to offer a gift of free and discounted books directly to your inbox. All you need to do is fill in the box below with your email address and name to start getting amazing offers in the comfort of your own home. You will never miss an offer because a reminder will be sent to you. Never miss a deal and get great deals without having to leave the house! Subscribe now and start saving!

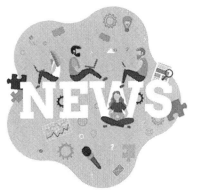

SUBSCRIBE
TO NEWSLETTER

Enter your email address

https://valeria-ray.gr8.com

Contents

Simple and Delicious Meal in a Mug Recipes

MMMMMMMMMMMMMMMMMMMMMMMMMMMMMM

Chapter I – Breakfast Recipes

MMMMMMMMMMMMMMMMMMMMMMMMMMMMMMMMM

(1) Ham, Mushroom and Swiss Cheese Scramble

Begin the day with a protein-rich breakfast. There really is no excuse when a healthy breakfast can be prepared in just four minutes.

Yield: 1

Cooking Time: 4mins

List of Ingredients:

- Nonstick cooking spray
- 1 medium egg
- 1 tablespoon water
- ¼ cup mushrooms (chopped)
- 1 ounce deli ham (chopped)
- 2 tablespoons Swiss cheese (shredded)

MMMMMMMMMMMMMMMMMMMMMMMMMMMMMMMM

Methods:

1. Spritz a large, microwave-safe mug with nonstick spray.
2. Add the egg, water, chopped mushrooms and deli ham, beating until thoroughly blended.
3. On high, microwave for 30 seconds and stir to combine.
4. Microwave for an additional 30-45 seconds until the egg is nearly set.
5. Season and top with shredded cheese.
6. Serve.

(2) Sweet Potato Hash

Not only are sweet potatoes delicious, but they are also rich in vitamins and minerals.

Yield: 1

Cooking Time: 10mins

List of Ingredients:

- 1 (6 ounce) sweet potato (peeled, diced)
- Water
- 1 tablespoon diced red onion
- 2 peppers (seeded, chopped)
- 2 tablespoons Cheddar cheese (grated)
- Pinch salt and black pepper
- ¼ tablespoons butter
- 2 teaspoons fresh rosemary

MMMMMMMMMMMMMMMMMMMMMMMMMMMMMMMM

Methods:

1. Add the potato to a large mug and cover with water.
2. Cook in the microwave for 3-4 minutes until soft. Stir halfway through cooking.
3. Drain away the water and add the onion, pepper, cheese, seasoning, butter, and rosemary, stirring well to combine.
4. Return to the microwave for 35-50 seconds until the cheddar melts. Serve.

(3) Breakfast Burrito

A filling breakfast burrito filled with protein-rich egg, beans, and cheddar will keep you feeling full till lunch.

Yield: 1

Cooking Time: 6mins

List of Ingredients:

- 1 large flour tortilla
- 2 medium eggs (beaten)
- Salt and black pepper
- 2 tablespoons shredded Cheddar cheese
- 2 tablespoons black beans
- 2 tablespoons chopped scallions

MMMMMMMMMMMMMMMMMMMMMMMMMMMMMMMMMM

Methods:

1. Press the tortilla into a large mug, allowing the tortilla to naturally fold into a cup shape.
2. Season the beaten egg with salt and pepper then pour into the tortilla. Stir in the cheese, black beans, and scallions.
3. Cook in the microwave for 80-100 seconds until set. Allow to cool for a couple of minutes before serving.

(4) Whole Wheat Raisin and Banana Muffin

A wholesome and nutritious mug muffin is a tasty way to wake up!

Yield: 1

Cooking Time: 3mins

List of Ingredients:

- 3 tablespoons whole wheat flour
- ¼ teaspoons cinnamon
- ½ teaspoons baking powder
- 2" chunk ripe banana (mashed)
- Pinch salt
- 2½ tablespoons whole milk
- 2 teaspoons maple syrup
- 1 tablespoon raisins

MMMMMMMMMMMMMMMMMMMMMMMMMMMMMMMMMM

Methods:

1. Combine the flour, cinnamon, baking powder, mashed banana, salt, milk, and maple syrup in a large mug.
2. Stir in the raisins.
3. Cook in the microwave for 45-60 seconds until springy to the touch.

(5) Cheese and Ham Eggs

Fluffy scrambled eggs with gooey cheese and tasty pieces of ham is a simple, yet delicious meal that comes together in minutes.

Yield: 1

Cooking Time: 5mins

List of Ingredients:

- Nonstick cooking spray
- 2 medium eggs
- 1 teaspoon seasoning of choice
- 2 tablespoons Cheddar cheese (grated)
- 2 tablespoons deli counter ham (diced)

MMMMMMMMMMMMMMMMMMMMMMMMMMMMMMMMMM

Methods:

1. Spritz a mug with nonstick spray.
2. Add the eggs to the mug along with the seasoning and whisk to combine.
3. Stir in the cheese and ham.
4. Cook in the microwave for 90 seconds on high heat until set. Allow to cool a little before serving.

(6) Morning Mug Cookie

A warm oatmeal and raisin cookie naturally sweetened with honey is a delicious way to start the day!

Yield: 1

Cooking Time: 3mins

List of Ingredients:

- 1½ tablespoons smooth peanut butter
- ½ ripe banana (mashed)
- 1 tablespoon whole milk
- ½ tablespoons honey
- 1 tablespoon raisins
- 4 tablespoons rolled oats

MMMMMMMMMMMMMMMMMMMMMMMMMMMMM

Methods:

1. Combine the peanut butter, mashed banana, milk, and honey in a large mug.
2. Stir in the raisins and oats.
3. Cook in the microwave for 50-60 minutes until springy to the touch.
4. Serve warm.

(7) Shakshuka

A Middle Eastern breakfast dish combining eggs, rich tomato sauce, and aromatic spices.

Yield: 1

Cooking Time: 4mins

List of Ingredients:

- ½ cup tomato sauce
- 1 teaspoon cumin
- ½ teaspoons each garlic powder, onion powder, red pepper flakes, oregano
- 1 large egg

MMMMMMMMMMMMMMMMMMMMMMMMMMMMMM

Methods:

1. Combine the tomato sauce and spices in a large mug.
2. Make a well in the tomato sauce, crack the egg into the well.
3. Place in the microwave and cook in 30-second intervals for approximately 2½ minutes. The egg white should be fully cooked.
4. Serve.

(8) Coconut Flour Pancake

Top this fluffy coconut flour pancake with fresh fruits, syrup or even whipped cream.

Yield: 1

Cooking Time: 3mins

List of Ingredients:

- 1 tablespoon butter (melted)
- 2 tablespoons Greek yogurt
- 2 tablespoons coconut flour
- 1 medium egg
- 1 tablespoon skim milk
- Fresh fruit (chopped)
- Maple syrup

MMMMMMMMMMMMMMMMMMMMMMMMMMMMMMMMM

Methods:

1. Swirl the melted butter around a large mug.
2. Add the remaining ingredients to the mug (yogurt, flour, egg, milk) and whisk to combine with a fork.
3. Cook in the microwave for 60-90 seconds until set.
4. Top with fresh fruit and maple syrup.

(9) Roasted Red Pepper and Feta Omelet

A protein-rich omelet filled with sweet roasted red peppers and salty feta cheese.

Yield: 1

Cooking Time: 4mins

List of Ingredients:

- Nonstick cooking spray
- 2 medium eggs
- ¼ cup fresh spinach
- 1 tablespoon roasted red pepper (diced)
- 1 teaspoon scallions (sliced)
- 1 tablespoon feta (crumbled)
- Salt and pepper (to taste)

MMMMMMMMMMMMMMMMMMMMMMMMMMMMMMM

Methods:

1. Spritz a large mug with nonstick spray.
2. Beat the eggs using a fork and stir in the spinach, pepper, scallion, feta, and a pinch of seasoning.
3. Cook on high heat for 90 seconds.
4. Allow to cool for 60 seconds before serving.

(10) Dark Choc Chip and Pecan Banana Bread

Moist and fluffy banana bread with melting chocolate chips and crunchy pecan pieces is a breakfast-time indulgence.

Yield: 1

Cooking Time: 6mins

List of Ingredients:

- 2 tablespoons brown sugar
- ¼ teaspoons baking powder
- 2 tablespoons coconut flour
- ½ banana (mashed)
- ¼ cup almond butter
- ¼ cup unsweetened coconut milk
- 2 teaspoons finely chopped pecans
- 1 tablespoon dark choc chips

MMMMMMMMMMMMMMMMMMMMMMMMMMMMMMMM

Methods:

1. Combine the sugar, baking powder, and flour in a small bowl.
2. In a second bowl, combine the mashed banana, almond butter, and coconut milk.
3. Add the wet mixture to the dry mixture and stir to combine. Transfer the mixture to a large mug. Stir in the chopped pecans and choc chips.
4. Pop in the microwave and cook for approximately 2½ minutes until firm.

(11) Pumpkin Breakfast Quinoa

Quinoa is high in protein, gluten-free, and contains all nine essential amino acids, not to mention fiber and antioxidants. Your body will thank you for incorporating this superfood into your diet.

Yield: 1

Cooking Time: 5mins

List of Ingredients:

- ⅓ cup pureed pumpkin
- ⅓ cup cooked quinoa
- ¼ teaspoons salt
- 2 medium eggs
- 1 tablespoon maple syrup
- ¼ teaspoons pumpkin pie spice

MMMMMMMMMMMMMMMMMMMMMMMMMMMMMMM

Methods:

1. Combine the pureed pumpkin, quinoa, salt, eggs, maple syrup, and spice in a bowl.
2. Transfer to a large mug and place in the microwave. Cook for approximately 3 minutes until set.

(12) French Toast

Who doesn't love biting into soft, cinnamon-spiced French toast in the morning?

Yield: 1

Cooking Time: 4mins

List of Ingredients:

- 1 tablespoon butter (melted)
- 1 medium egg (lightly beaten)
- ¼ cup whole milk
- ¼ teaspoons sugar
- ¼ teaspoons cinnamon
- ¼ teaspoons vanilla essence
- 2 slices white bread (sliced into cubes)

MMMMMMMMMMMMMMMMMMMMMMMMMMMMMMMM

Methods:

1. Swirl the melted butter around a large mug.
2. Add the egg, milk, sugar, cinnamon, and vanilla essence to the mug whisking to combine.
3. Add the bread to the mug and press down on the cubes to soak them in the liquid.
4. Place in the microwave and cook for 90 seconds, until set.

(13) PB&J Oatmeal

Your favorite sandwich filling is transformed into a delicious filling oatmeal.

Yield: 1

Cooking Time: 5mins

List of Ingredients:

- 6 tablespoons water
- 3 tablespoons rolled oats
- 2 teaspoons almond milk
- 2 teaspoons grape jelly
- 2 teaspoons creamy peanut butter

MMMMMMMMMMMMMMMMMMMMMMMMMMMMMM

Methods:

1. Combine the water, oats, and milk in a large mug. Stir in the jelly and peanut butter.
2. Cook in the microwave for 3 minutes, removing every 60 seconds to stir.
3. Allow to cool for 30 seconds before serving.

(14) Iced Cinnamon Roll

A soft cinnamon spiced roll drizzled with sticky sweet icing is a true breakfast-time indulgence.

Yield: 1

Cooking Time: 4mins

List of Ingredients:

Cinnamon Roll:

- 1 medium egg
- 2 tablespoons milk
- ½ teaspoons vanilla essence
- 1 tablespoon melted butter
- 1½ tablespoons maple syrup
- 1 teaspoon cinnamon
- 2 tablespoons coconut flour
- Pinch nutmeg
- Pinch sea salt
- ½ teaspoons baking powder

Icing:

- 1 tablespoon coconut butter
- 1 tablespoon almond milk
- 1 teaspoon coconut sugar
- ½ teaspoons lemon juice

MMMMMMMMMMMMMMMMMMMMMMMMMMMMMMM

Methods:

1. Whisk together the egg, milk, vanilla, melted butter, and maple syrup in a microwave-safe mug.
2. In a small bowl, combine the cinnamon, flour, nutmeg, salt, and baking powder. Whisk this mixture into the wet ingredients.
3. Cook in the microwave for 2 minutes. In the meantime, whisk together all of the icing ingredients (coconut butter, milk, sugar, lemon juice) until smooth.
4. Drizzle the prepared icing over the cooked cinnamon roll and serve.

Chapter II – Main Recipes

MMMMMMMMMMMMMMMMMMMMMMMMMMMMMMMMM

(15) Thai Green Curry

Forget the expensive take-out, instead reach for your favorite mug, add a handful of ingredients, and wait for that ping.

Yield: 1

Cooking Time: 7mins

List of Ingredients:

- ½ cup coconut milk
- 1 teaspoon green curry paste
- 3 tablespoons peas (frozen)
- Handful of vermicelli rice noodles
- 1 tablespoon freshly squeezed lime juice
- Cilantro (to garnish)
- Red chili (sliced, to garnish)

MMMMMMMMMMMMMMMMMMMMMMMMMMMMMMMMM

Methods:

1. Add the coconut milk, green curry paste, fresh lime juice and peas to a large, microwave-safe mug.
2. Stir to combine and add the noodles.
3. On high, microwave for 1½-2 minutes, depending on your appliance wattage, until the noodles are fully cooked and soft.
4. Stir, allow to cool a little, garnish with red chili and enjoy.

(16) Calzone

You don't need to travel to Naples to enjoy this folded pizza, now you can enjoy a taste of Italy in just five minutes.

Yield: 1

Cooking Time: 5mins

List of Ingredients:

- 8 tablespoons all-purpose flour
- ⅛ teaspoons baking soda
- ¼ teaspoons baking powder
- ¼ teaspoons salt
- 6 tablespoons milk
- 2 tablespoons olive oil
- 2-3 tablespoons tomato sauce (divided)
- 4-5 tablespoons mozzarella cheese (finely grated)
- ¼ teaspoons dry Italian seasoning
- Parsley (to garnish)

MMMMMMMMMMMMMMMMMMMMMMMMMMMMMM

Methods:

1. In a mug, combine the flour with the baking soda, baking powder and salt.
2. Add the milk along with the oil and mix to a silky smooth batter.
3. In the middle of the batter, drop one spoonful of the tomato sauce, grated cheese, and seasoning.
4. Carefully pull the batter over the fillings to hide under the batter.
5. Microwave on high for 1 min 50 secs to 2 mins 10 secs until the surface of the calzone is firm to the touch and risen. Timings will depend on the wattage of your microwave.
6. Garnish with parsley and additional tomato sauce and enjoy.

(17) Spinach and Cheddar Quiche

Who needs an oven? All you need to make this meal is a microwave and a mug.

Yield: 1

Cooking Time: 5mins

List of Ingredients:

- ½ cup frozen spinach (thawed, drained, chopped)
- 1 medium egg
- ⅓ cup whole milk
- ⅓ cup Cheddar cheese (shredded)
- 1 rasher cooked bacon (chopped small)
- Salt and black pepper

MMMMMMMMMMMMMMMMMMMMMMMMMMMMMMM

Methods:

1. Add the thawed spinach to a microwave-safe mug.
2. Crack the egg into the mug and add the whole milk followed by the cheese and bacon. Season with salt and black pepper, mixing thoroughly until incorporated.
3. Cove the mug with a kitchen paper towel and on high, microwave for a few minutes, until fluffy and cooked through.

(18) Chicken Pie in a Mug

A wholesome chicken pie in a mug is a mouth-watering meal in a mug.

Yield: 1

Cooking Time: 10mins

List of Ingredients:

- 3-4 tablespoons cooked chicken
- 2 tablespoons frozen vegetables
- 1½ teaspoons cornstarch
- Salt and black pepper
- 3 tablespoons chicken stock
- 1 tablespoon full-fat milk

Biscuit topping:

- 4 tablespoons flour
- ½ teaspoons baking powder
- ⅛ teaspoons salt
- ½ tablespoons butter (cut into cubes)
- 3½ tablespoons whole milk
- 1 tablespoon herbs (chopped)

MMMMMMMMMMMMMMMMMMMMMMMMMMMMMMM

Methods:

1. In a microwave-safe mug, add the cooked chicken with the frozen veggies, cornstarch, salt, and pepper. Stir to combine.
2. Add the stock along with the milk, stirring thoroughly until all the ingredients are combined. Set to one side.
3. To make the topping, combine the flour with the baking powder and salt.
4. With a fork, rub in the cubes of butter until the consistency of fine breadcrumbs.
5. Stir in the milk followed by the herbs, to form a batter.
6. Scoop the batter on top of the chicken mixture.
7. Microwave for between 2-2¼ minutes, depending on your microwave wattage, or until the batter is firm.
8. Serve.

(19) Spicy Bean Chilli

Generally, chili takes hours to prepare on the stove, but now you can enjoy this spicy chili from mug to microwave in just six minutes.

Yield: 1

Cooking Time: 6mins

List of Ingredients:

- 3 tablespoons red kidney beans
- 3 tablespoons corn
- 3 tablespoons carrots (finely chopped)
- 1 tablespoon onion (peeled, finely chopped)
- 6 tablespoons tomato sauce
- ½ teaspoons cumin
- ½ teaspoons chili powder
- 1 teaspoon Worcestershire sauce
- ½ teaspoons Tabasco sauce

Toppings (optional):

- Sour cream
- Avocado (peeled, pitted, diced)

MMMMMMMMMMMMMMMMMMMMMMMMMMMMMMMMM

Methods:

1. In a microwave-safe mug, combine the kidney beans with the corn, carrots, onion, tomato sauce, cumin, chili powder, Worcestershire sauce and Tabasco.
2. Microwave for 2-2 ½ minutes.
3. Serve with your favorite toppings.

(20) Creamy Fettuccine Alfredo

Pasta in a mug in a creamy sauce, topped with Parmesan is the ideal meal for either lunch or dinner.

Yield: 1

Cooking Time: 14mins

List of Ingredients:

- 2 ounces fettuccine pasta (cooked)
- 1 tablespoon butter
- ¼ cup heavy cream
- 3 tablespoons Parmesan cheese (grated)
- ¼ teaspoons garlic powder
- Parmesan cheese (to garnish)
- Salt and black pepper

MMMMMMMMMMMMMMMMMMMMMMMMMMMMMMMM

Methods:

1. Cook the pasta according to the manufacturer's instructions and until al dente. Drain and allow to cool.
2. In a microwave-safe mug, combine the cooked pasta with the butter, cream, grated cheese, and garlic powder.
3. Transfer to the microwave for 90 seconds.
4. Stir to incorporate and top with additional Parmesan, season and enjoy.

(21) Ramen

In just five minutes you can be enjoying a flavorsome Asian-inspired meal.

Yield: 1

Cooking Time: 5mins

List of Ingredients:

- 1 cup chicken stock
- ¼ portion ramen noodles
- 2 tablespoons frozen mixed vegetables
- 2 teaspoons soy sauce
- ½ teaspoons chili sauce
- 1 tablespoon green onions (sliced)
- Sesame seeds (to garnish)
- Chili sauce (to serve)

MMMMMMMMMMMMMMMMMMMMMMMMMMMMMMM

Methods:

1. In a large, microwave-safe mug combine the chicken stock, ramen noodles, veggies, soy sauce, chili sauce, and onions. Breaking up the noodles, so they fit easily in the mug.
2. Microwave for 2-2 ½ minutes, until the noodles are bite tender. Timings will depend on the wattage of your microwave.
3. Serve, garnished with sesame seeds and drizzled with additional chili sauce.

(22) Fish Pie

A romantic meal for two in less than 40 minutes? Then this creamy fish pie is sure to be top of the menu.

Yield: 2

Cooking Time: 35mins

List of Ingredients:

Potatoes:

- 14 ounces white potatoes
- 2 ½ ounces milk
- 1 tablespoon butter
- 1 teaspoon lemon zest
- 1 teaspoon toasted fennel seeds

Filling:

- 1 tablespoon butter
- 2½ ounces white wine
- ¼ leek (washed, cut into quarters lengthwise, sliced)
- ½ garlic cloves (peeled, minced)
- 5 ounces mixed fish
- 1 teaspoon Dijon mustard
- 3⅓ ounces double cream
- 1 tablespoon fresh chives (chopped)

Toppings:

- 5 teaspoons Cheddar cheese (grated)
- 2 teaspoons pine nuts
- 3 teaspoons almond flakes

Methods:

1. On full power, microwave the potatoes in a microwave-safe bowl for 10 minutes of full power.
2. Scrape the flesh out of the potato skins and add to the bowl. Add the milk followed by the butter and mash to combine. Add the lemon zest followed by the fennel seeds, gently stirring without over-mixing.
3. To 2 large mugs, add the butter, wine, leeks and garlic and on high power, microwave for 5 minutes.
4. Add the fish along with the Dijon mustard, cream, and chives to the mugs and stir.
5. Layer the potato on top of the fish and fish with the grated Cheddar cheese along with the pine nuts and almond flakes.
6. Microwave for an additional 10 minutes, until piping hot and browned.
7. Wearing oven gloves remove from the microwave, allow to cool a little and serve.

(23) Pulled Pork Pies

It takes only four ingredients and seven minutes for you to be enjoying and sharing a tasty and satisfying meal in a mug.

Yield: 2

Cooking Time: 7mins

List of Ingredients:

- 1 pound cooked pulled pork
- 1 cup mixed vegetables (frozen)
- 24 ounces mashed potatoes
- ½ cup Cheddar cheese (shredded)

MMMMMMMMMMMMMMMMMMMMMMMMMMMMMMMM

Methods:

1. Layer the pork, veggies, and mash in 4 large coffee mugs. Top with an equal amount of shredded cheese.
2. On high, microwave for 2 minutes.
3. Allow to cool slightly and serve.

(24) Mac 'n Mug Cheese

You are just seven minutes away from a single serving of one of your favorite go-to meals.

Yield: 1

Cooking Time: 7mins

List of Ingredients:

- ⅓ cup small elbow macaroni noodles (uncooked)
- ½ cup water
- ¼ cup whole milk
- ½ cup Cheddar cheese (finely shredded)

MMMMMMMMMMMMMMMMMMMMMMMMMMMMMMMM

Methods:

1. Add the macaroni and cold water to a microwave-safe mug.
2. On full power, microwave for 2 minutes. Stirring to combine.
3. Microwave for an additional 60 seconds and stir.
4. Microwave for a further 60 seconds and stir. If the water is not entirely absorbed, microwave for a few more seconds.
5. Stir in the milk and Cheddar cheese and microwave for between 30-60 seconds.
6. Stir, allow to cool a little and enjoy.

(25) Pepperoni Pizza

Say goodbye to fast food and instead take 5 minutes out to microwave this spicy Italian-style pizza.

Yield: 1

Cooking Time: 5mins

List of Ingredients:

- ⅛ teaspoons baking powder
- 4 tablespoons all-purpose flour
- Pinch of baking soda
- 3 tablespoons whole milk
- ⅛ teaspoons salt
- 1 tablespoon olive oil
- 1 tablespoon marinara sauce
- 1 tablespoon mozzarella cheese (shredded)
- 5 mini-pepperoni
- ½ teaspoons dried Italian herbs

MMMMMMMMMMMMMMMMMMMMMMMMMMMMMMM

Methods:

1. In a mug, combine the flour with the baking powder, soda and salt and stir to combine.
2. Add the milk and olive oil, mixing to combine.
3. Spoon on the marinara sauce, evenly spreading it on the surface of the batter.
4. Scatter with the mozzarella, mini-pepperoni, and herbs.
5. On high, microwave for 60-90 seconds, until the top bubbles.
6. Enjoy.

(26) Meat Loaf in a Mug

A classic, all-time favorite dish with the minimum of clean-up is the perfect midweek meal.

Yield: 1

Cooking Time: 15mins

List of Ingredients:

- 2 tablespoons 2% milk
- 1 tablespoon ketchup
- 2 tablespoons quick-cooking oats
- 1 teaspoon onion soup mix
- ¼ pound lean ground beef
- Nonstick cooking spray
- Ketchup (to serve)

MMMMMMMMMMMMMMMMMMMMMMMMMMMMMMMM

Methods:

1. In a mixing bowl, add the 2% milk to the ketchup, quick-cooking oats, and onion soup mix.
2. Crumble the ground beef over the top and mix to combine.
3. Add to a microwave-safe mug coated with nonstick cooking spray.
4. Cove the mug and on high, microwave for a few minutes, until the beef is no longer pink and an internal thermometer registers 160 degrees. Drain.
5. Set aside to cool for a few minutes and serve with tomato ketchup.

Chapter III – Dessert Recipes

MMMMMMMMMMMMMMMMMMMMMMMMMMMMMMMMM

(27) White Chocolate Chip Blondie

Scrummy white chocolate chip blondies are sure to hit your sweet spot. So, kick off your shoes, put up your feet and enjoy.

Yield: 1

Cooking Time: 12mins

List of Ingredients:

- 2 tablespoons butter
- 3 tablespoons brown sugar
- 3 tablespoons whole milk
- ½ teaspoons vanilla essence
- 6 tablespoons flour
- ⅛ teaspoons salt
- ⅛ teaspoons baking powder
- 1 tablespoon white chocolate chips
- 4 caramel candies (chopped)
- Ice cream (to serve)

MMMMMMMMMMMMMMMMMMMMMMMMMMMMMMM

Methods:

1. In a microwave-safe mug, melt the butter.
2. Add the sugar followed by the milk and vanilla essence and mix until the sugar is entirely dissolved.
3. A little at a time stir in the flour, salt, and baking powder, mixing until incorporated.
4. Add the chocolate chips along with the caramel candies.
5. Cover and transfer to the refrigerator for up to 48 hours.
6. When you are ready to serve, microwave on full power for 80 seconds, check the blondie's progress and return to the microwave to cook for 30 seconds.
7. Serve with ice cream.

(28) Angel Cake

A heavenly low carb, gluten-free cake that you can enjoy guilt-free.

Yield: 1

Cooking Time: 3mins

List of Ingredients:

- 2 tablespoons coconut flour
- 2 tablespoons granulated sweetener
- ⅛ teaspoons salt
- ¼ teaspoons baking powder
- 2 large eggs
- 2 tablespoons almond milk
- 1½ tablespoons unsalted butter
- ¼ teaspoons vanilla essence

MMMMMMMMMMMMMMMMMMMMMMMMMMMMMMMMMM

Methods:

1. In a mug, combine the flour, sweetener, salt and baking powder, mixing to combine.
2. Add the eggs, milk, butter, and essence, mixing until incorporated.
3. Microwave on full power for between 60-90 seconds or until sufficiently cooked.

(29) Strawberry Puff Pies

Flaky puff pastry filled with fresh strawberries and baked until golden makes an ideal fuss-free, family dessert choice.

Yield: 4

Cooking Time: 50mins

List of Ingredients:

- 2 pounds fresh strawberries (hulled, quartered)
- 2 tablespoons granulated sugar
- 1 tablespoon all-purpose flour
- Pinch of salt
- 1 puff pastry sheet (thawed, cut into 4 circles)
- 1 medium egg (lightly beaten)

MMMMMMMMMMMMMMMMMMMMMMMMMMMMMMMM

Methods:

1. Preheat the main oven to 400 degrees F.
2. In a casserole dish, combine the strawberries with the sugar, flour, and salt, mixing to combine.
3. Divide the mixture into 4 microwave-safe mugs.
4. Arrange the circles of puff pastry, one on top of each mug and lightly wash with beaten egg.
5. Place the 4 mugs on a cookie sheet and transfer to the oven for 25-30 minutes, checking halfway through to stir the strawberries and check on the pastry's progress.
6. When the pastry is puffed and golden, remove from the oven and allow to cool for 4-5 minutes.
7. Serve.

(30) Apple Crisp

Fast and fruity, delicious apple with crisp oats is the ideal dessert to satisfy those sweet cravings.

Yield: 1

Cooking Time: 3mins

List of Ingredients:

- 1 small gala apple (peeled, cored, sliced)
- 2 teaspoons granulated sugar
- 1 teaspoon cinnamon (divided)
- ¼ cup oats
- 2 tablespoons flour
- 2 tablespoons brown sugar
- 2 tablespoons butter (melted)

MMMMMMMMMMMMMMMMMMMMMMMMMMMMMMMMMM

Methods:

1. In a microwave-safe, small bowl combine the slices of apples with the sugar and ½ teaspoon of cinnamon.
2. Combine the oats with the flour, sugar and remaining cinnamon.
3. Add the melted butter, stirring to incorporate.
4. Top the apples with the oat-cinnamon mixture.
5. Microwave on high power for between 1½-2 minutes, until crisp.
6. Carefully remove from the microwave and top with ice cream or whipped cream.

(31) Red Velvet Mug Cake

This classic red velvet cake with a sweet and creamy frosting is perfect with a cup of hot tea or coffee.

Yield: 1-2

Cooking Time: 5mins

List of Ingredients:

Cake:

- 4 tablespoons flour
- 4½ tablespoons white sugar
- ⅛ teaspoons baking powder
- 1½ tablespoons unsweetened cocoa powder
- 3 tablespoons canola oil
- 3 tablespoons buttermilk
- 1 medium egg
- ½ teaspoons red food gel

Frosting:

- 2 tablespoons cream cheese
- 2 tablespoons butter
- ½ cup sugar

MMMMMMMMMMMMMMMMMMMMMMMMMMMMMMMM

Methods:

1. In a large mug, combine the flour, sugar, baking powder, cocoa powder, oil, buttermilk, egg, and food coloring, using a fork to whisk until silky smooth.

2. Cook for 90 seconds in the microwave, check if cooked through and if not return to the microwave for an additional 30 seconds.

3. Allow the cake to slightly cool, before frosting.

4. To prepare the frosting, while the cake cools, combine the cream cheese with the butter and sugar and on high speed, mix until fluffy.

5. Spread or pipe onto the cake.

(32) Blueberry Cake

A berrylicious mug cake will tick all the boxes and satisfy all those sweet cravings.

Yield: 1

Cooking Time: 5mins

List of Ingredients:

- 4 tablespoons all-purpose flour
- ¼ teaspoons baking powder
- 2½ teaspoons granulated sugar
- 3 tablespoons fat-free milk
- ½ tablespoons vegetable oil
- ¼ teaspoons vanilla essence
- 10 fresh blueberries (washed, dried)

MMMMMMMMMMMMMMMMMMMMMMMMMMMMMMMMMM

Methods:

1. Combine the flour, baking powder, sugar, milk, oil, and essence in an extra-large, microwave-safe mug, mixing with a whisk until the batter is silky smooth.
2. Fold in the berries, making sure they are not on top of the batter but incorporated throughout.
3. Cook on high in the microwave for between 60-90 seconds, until fully cooked.
4. Allow to cool for 2-3 minutes and enjoy warm.

(33) Pumpkin Pie

Winter or shine, this pie is the quintessential comfort food.

Yield: 1

Cooking Time: 5mins

List of Ingredients:

Crust:

- 1 tablespoon butter
- 1 tablespoon shredded coconut
- 1 tablespoon almond flour

Topping:

- ½ cup pumpkin puree
- 1 medium egg
- 1 teaspoon pumpkin pie spice
- 2 tablespoons maple syrup

MMMMMMMMMMMMMMMMMMMMMMMMMMMMMMM

Methods:

1. First, make the crust. Add the butter to a large ramekin and melt in the microwave, this will take approximately 30 seconds.
2. Add the shredded coconut and the flour to the melted butter and combine with a spoon, while patting it down gently to form a crust.
3. In a second bowl, combine the pumpkin puree with the egg, pumpkin spice, and maple syrup, mixing until silky smooth.
4. Pour the mixture over the crust in the ramekin.
5. Transfer to the microwave for a couple of minutes before checking to see if the middle is wet. If it is, return to the microwave for an additional 20-30 seconds.
6. Allow to cool before adding your favorite toppings and enjoy.

(34) Brown Sugar Spice Mug Cake

A moist cake with homemade cream cheese frosting in just over five minutes has to be the best-ever dessert ever.

Yield: 1

Cooking Time: 6mins

List of Ingredients:

Cream cheese icing:

- 1 tablespoon cream cheese (softened)
- 2 tablespoons confectioner's sugar
- 1 teaspoon milk

Cake:

- 2 tablespoons organic applesauce
- 1 tablespoon canola oil
- 1 tablespoon buttermilk
- ¼ teaspoons vanilla essence
- ¼ cup + 1 tablespoon all-purpose flour
- 2½ tablespoons packed light brown sugar
- ¾ teaspoons ground cinnamon
- Pinch nutmeg
- ¼ teaspoons baking powder
- ⅛ teaspoons salt

MMMMMMMMMMMMMMMMMMMMMMMMMMMMMMMMM

Methods:

1. First, make the icing. Combine the cream cheese with the sugar and milk, whisking until combined and smooth.

2. To prepare the cheesecake, in a mug combine the applesauce, oil, buttermilk, essence, flour, light brown sugar, cinnamon, nutmeg, baking powder and salt and whisk until smooth.

3. Transfer the mug to the microwave and on high power, microwave for 60 seconds. Check to see is the cake is cooked and if it isn't microwave for another 15 seconds.

4. Serve the cake topped with the homemade cream cheese icing in a swirl pattern.

(35) Peach Cobbler

It's time to take time out and enjoy this peachy perfect cobbler, made in a mug in just six minutes.

Yield: 1

Cooking Time: 6mins

List of Ingredients:

- 1 tablespoon butter
- 3 tablespoons white cake mix
- 1 pinch cinnamon
- 1 pinch nutmeg
- 2½ tablespoons whole milk
- 1 (4 ounce) diced peaches in light syrup
- Ice cream

MMMMMMMMMMMMMMMMMMMMMMMMMMMMM

Methods:

1. Add the butter to a microwave-safe mug and in the microwave, melt.
2. In the meantime, in a bowl, whisk the cake mix with the cinnamon and nutmeg. Add the milk, stirring until incorporated.
3. Without stirring, pour the mixture over the melted butter in the mug.
4. Drain 2 tablespoons of peach liquid from the peaches and discard.
5. Without stirring, pour the remaining peaches over the top of the cake mix and, on half power, microwave for between 3-4 minutes, until cooked through.
6. Set aside to slightly cool, and top with ice cream.

(36) Cheesecake in a Mug

Spoil yourself with this single serving cheesecake. It's creamy, moreish and easy to make.

Yield: 1

Cooking Time: 1hour 10mins

List of Ingredients:

Crust:

- 4 tablespoons fine graham cracker crumbs
- 1 tablespoon melted butter

Cheesecake:

- 1 large egg (whisked)
- 4 tablespoons cream cheese (softened)
- 2 tablespoons plain nonfat Greek yogurt
- 2½ tablespoons granulated sugar
- ¼ teaspoons vanilla essence
- Few fresh raspberries (to garnish)

MMMMMMMMMMMMMMMMMMMMMMMMMMMMMMM

Methods:

1. Grease a microwave-safe mug on the interior, base, and sides.
2. Add the fine graham cracker crumbs and butter, mixing until combined.
3. Gently press the crumbs down to form a crust in the bottom of the greased mug.
4. In a bowl, add the egg with the cream cheese, Greek yogurt, sugar, and vanilla essence. Mix, using a whisk, until silky smooth.
5. Add the batter to the mug.
6. Place a piece of kitchen paper on top of the mug and microwave on full power, for 60 seconds or until most of the cake is cooked. Check and then microwave in 20-second intervals until cooked through.
7. The cheesecake should pull away from the sides of the mug quite easily. The best way to do this is to invert the cake on a plate and flip over.
8. Allow to cool for 2-3 minutes before transferring to the fridge to chill for 60 minutes.
9. When entirely chilled garnish with fresh raspberries.

(37) Lemon Cheesecake

Easy peasy lemon cheesy, this cheesecake is to die for!

Yield: 1

Cooking Time: 3mins

List of Ingredients:

- 2 ounces cream cheese (at room temperature)
- 2 tablespoons sour cream
- 1 medium egg
- ½ teaspoons freshly squeezed lemon juice
- ¼ teaspoons vanilla essence
- 2-4 tablespoons sugar substitute

MMMMMMMMMMMMMMMMMMMMMMMMMMMMMMMMM

Methods:

1. In a microwave-safe mixing bowl combine the cream cheese with the sour cream, egg, lemon juice, vanilla essence and sugar substitute.
2. In the microwave, cook on high heat for 90 seconds, while stirring every 30 seconds.
3. Transfer to the fridge, to chill.

(38) Chocolate Brownie

Cuddle-up with this decadent and gooey chocolate brownie to share.

Yield: 1-2

Cooking Time: 2mins

List of Ingredients:

- ¼ cup all-purpose flour
- ¼ cup brown sugar
- 2 tablespoons unsweetened cocoa powder
- Pinch kosher salt
- 2 tablespoons canola oil
- 2 tablespoons whole milk
- 2 tablespoons dark chocolate (chopped)

MMMMMMMMMMMMMMMMMMMMMMMMMMMMMMMMM

Methods:

1. In a mug, combine the flour, sugar, cocoa powder and salt, until lump-free.
2. Stir in the canola oil and milk until a thick paste consistency.
3. Stir in the chopped dark chocolate until combined.
4. On high, microwave in 30-second intervals, until springy to the touch. This will take approximately 1 minute.

(39) Fudgy Mug Brownie

There really is nothing as gooey and delicious than a fudgy brownie topped with ice cream.

Yield: 1

Cooking Time: 2mins

List of Ingredients:

- Nonstick baking spray
- ¼ cup all-purpose flour
- ¼ cup granulated sugar
- 2 tablespoons cocoa powder
- Pinch salt
- 2 tablespoons whole milk
- 2 tablespoons vegetable oil
- 2 tablespoons chocolate chips

MMMMMMMMMMMMMMMMMMMMMMMMMMMMMMMM

Methods:

1. Spritz a mug with baking spray.
2. Add the flour, sugar, cocoa powder and salt to a bowl and mix to incorporate.
3. Add the whole milk, vegetable oil, and chocolate chips.
4. Stir the mixture until combined.
5. On a high setting, microwave for 60-90 seconds, or until sufficiently cooked.
6. Serve with ice cream and enjoy.

(40) Fig and Cardamom Cake

Fig and cardamom are the perfect pairings for this fabulous and fruity dessert in a mug.

Yield: 1

Cooking Time: 5mins

List of Ingredients:

- Nonstick baking spray
- 2 large figs (sliced crosswise)
- 4 teaspoons sweetener (divided)
- 2 tablespoons vanilla protein powder
- ¼ cup gluten-free baking blend
- ¼ teaspoons baking soda
- ¼ teaspoons ground cardamom
- ¼ teaspoons ground cinnamon
- ¼ teaspoons ground cloves
- 1 large egg
- 6 tablespoons unsweetened vanilla almond milk
- Greek yogurt (to serve)

MMMMMMMMMMMMMMMMMMMMMMMMMMMMMMM

Methods:

1. Spritz a 16-ounce mug with nonstick baking spray.

2. Arrange the figs in the bottom of the mug and halfway up the mug's sides.

3. Drizzle the figs with 1 teaspoon of sweetener. Set to one side.

4. In a bowl, combine the vanilla protein powder, baking mix, baking soda, cardamom, cinnamon, and cloves, stirring well until incorporated.

5. Combine the egg and milk in a second bowl. Add the wet mixture to the dry mixture and stir to combine.

6. Pour the mixture into the mug and over the figs.

7. Cook in the microwave for between 60-90 seconds, until cooked through. The cake is ready when it rises above the mug's rim and then fall once taken out of the microwave.

8. Remove from the microwave and invert onto a dinner plate, and gently slide out the mug cake.

9. Allow to cool for a couple of minutes.

10. Top with yogurt and enjoy.

About the Author

A native of Indianapolis, Indiana, Valeria Ray found her passion for cooking while she was studying English Literature at Oakland City University. She decided to try a cooking course with her friends and the experience changed her forever. She enrolled at the Art Institute of Indiana which offered extensive courses in the culinary Arts. Once Ray dipped her toe in the cooking world, she never looked back.

When Valeria graduated, she worked in French restaurants in the Indianapolis area until she became the head chef at one of the 5-star establishments in the area. Valeria's attention to taste and visual detail caught the eye of a local business person who expressed an interest in publishing her recipes. Valeria began her secondary career authoring cookbooks and e-books which she tackled with as much talent and gusto as her first career. Her passion for food leaps off the page of her books which have colourful anecdotes and stunning pictures of dishes she has prepared herself.

Valeria Ray lives in Indianapolis with her husband of 15 years, Tom, her daughter, Isobel and their loveable Golden Retriever, Goldy. Valeria enjoys cooking special dishes in her large, comfortable kitchen where the family gets involved in preparing meals. This successful, dynamic chef is an inspiration to culinary students and novice cooks everywhere.

••••••••• ● ● ● ● ● ● ● •••••

Author's Afterthoughts

Thank you for Purchasing my book and taking the time to read it from front to back. I am always grateful when a reader chooses my work and I hope you enjoyed it!

With the vast selection available online, I am touched that you chose to be purchasing my work and take valuable time out of your life to read it. My hope is that you feel you made the right decision.

I very much would like to know what you thought of the book. Please take the time to write an honest and informative review on Amazon.com. Your experience and opinions will be of great benefit to me and those readers looking to make an informed choice.

With much thanks,

Valeria Ray

Printed in Great Britain
by Amazon

48776974R00064